CW00350807

ROCK & POP STUDIES PIANO

88 PROGRESSIVE STUDIES AND EXERCISES

Written by Lucy Holliday & Olly Weeks
Artwork by Kenosha Design

© 2015 by Faber Music Ltd
First published by Faber Music Ltd in 2015
Bloomsbury House
74-77 Great Russell Street
London WC1B 3DA

Printed in England by Caligraving Ltd
All rights reserved

This paper is 100% recyclable

ISBN: 0-571-53908-4
EAN: 978-0-571-53908-6

To buy Faber Music publications or to find out about the full range of titles
available, please contact your local music retailer or Faber Music sales enquiries:

Faber Music Limited, Burnt Mill, Elizabeth Way, Harlow CM20 2HX
Tel: +44 (0)1279 82 89 82
Fax: +44 (0)1279 82 89 83

1.

Here's an easy study to get started with. This is a very common chord sequence
in pop music and can be found in many songs. It's a great starter piece for
learning pop piano because your hands can stay in the same position throughout.

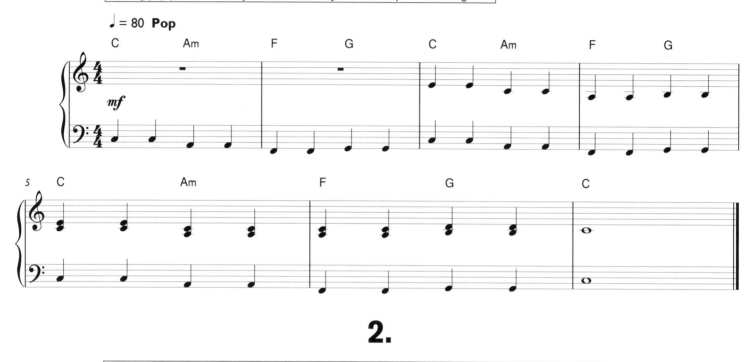

2.

A simple vamping exercise designed to teach the basic structure of the 12-bar blues.
Once you feel comfortable with this, experiment by adding a moving bass-line and solos in the right hand.

3.

Playing in 3 time gives rock & pop music a whole new feel. Pedalling at the start of every bar gives this piece just the right amount of sustain and reverb. It's left hand only for the first section, so keep looping this sequence until you're confident, then add the right-hand part. It's a perfect sequence to improvise over, so you could just use the melody as a starting point then do your own thing.

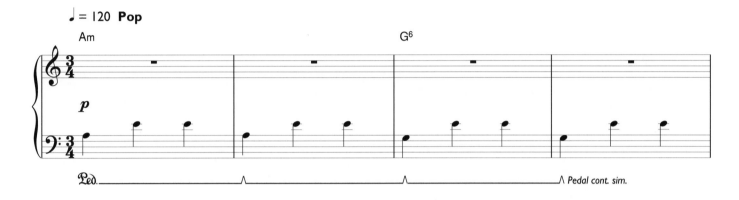

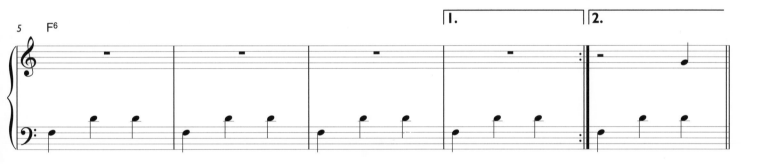

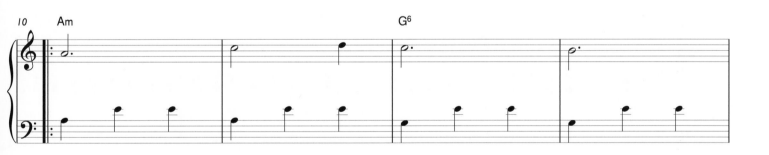

4

This style is extremely common in pop ballads and has a slight gospel feel to it.
The syncopated (off-beat) chords at the end of bars 1,3,5 & 7 create the feel of the whole piece.

♩ = 80 **Soul / gospel**

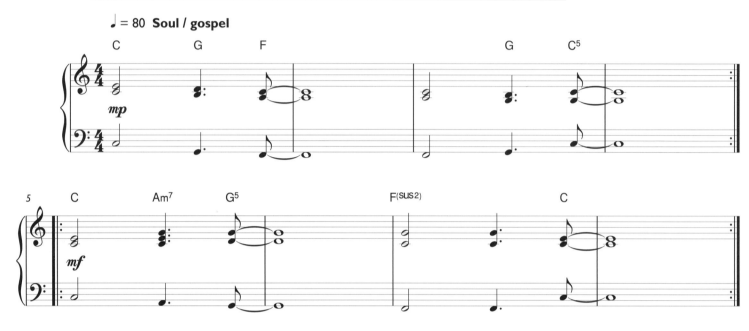

5.

Play the right-hand chords really lightly (no pedalling) and the left hand clearly.
This style of playing provides a typical accompaniment to many pop songs.

♩ = 80 **Pop**

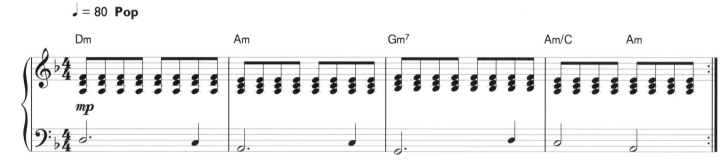

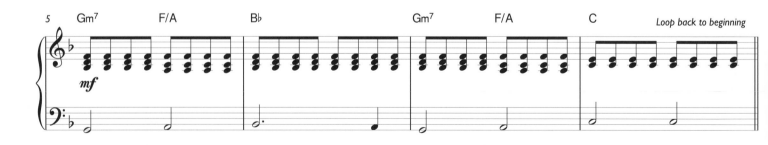

6.

This study is all about the left hand. There are staccato notes, accents and grace notes to look out for that help to give the piece a laid-back soul feel. Check out songs by Otis Redding, Bill Withers and Marvin Gaye for more inspiration.

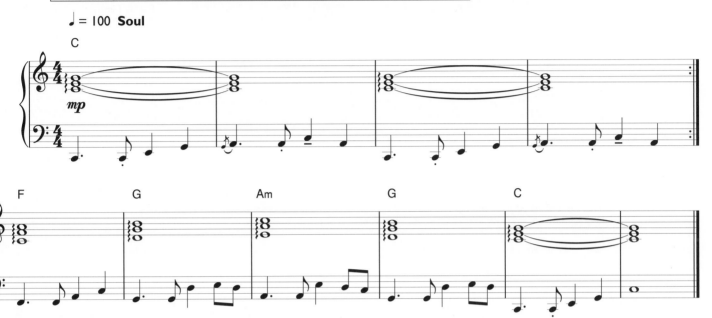

7.

This study uses syncopation in both hands at the same time.
It can be helpful to play with a metronome to hear where the beat falls.

6

8.

The feature of this study is the staccato chord on the off-beat of beat 3.
Take it steady and keep that chord really light. It adds a nice touch to a very simple progression.

9.

Your right hand plays on the beat in this study, whilst your left hand plays the syncopated, off-beat notes. Try playing it slowly at first to get used to the feel.

10.

All the chords in the right hand are played off-beat in this study.
This gives a basic reggae feel. Make sure you don't hold any of the notes on into the rests. No pedalling required!

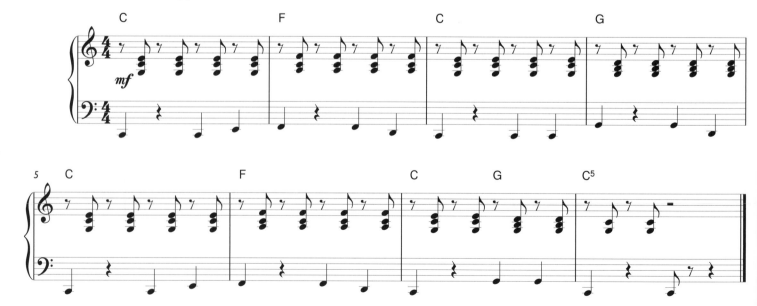

11.

This octave jumping left-hand part provides a classic bass-line, which enhances the drum pattern in pop songs. It's all about the bass in this study, keep it rhythmic and steady; if you're having trouble stretching the octave leap then play with a very light touch so you almost bounce off the keys in order to make the jump.

12.

As with much classical piano music, the arpeggio is frequently used in pop ballads. This can give quite a melancholic feel to a piece. Here, the left hand plays the root of the chords with the right hand extending the arpeggio afterwards.

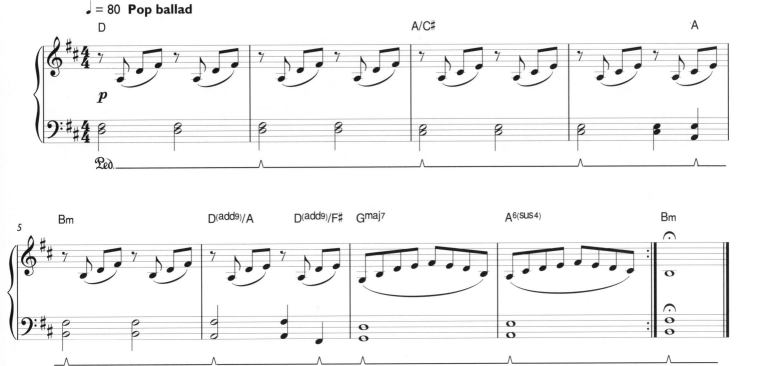

13.

This study is centred around intervals of thirds and fifths, with a couple of exceptions.
Take it slow and use the chord names as an easy guide to see where the harmony changes.

♩ = 70 **Pop ballad**

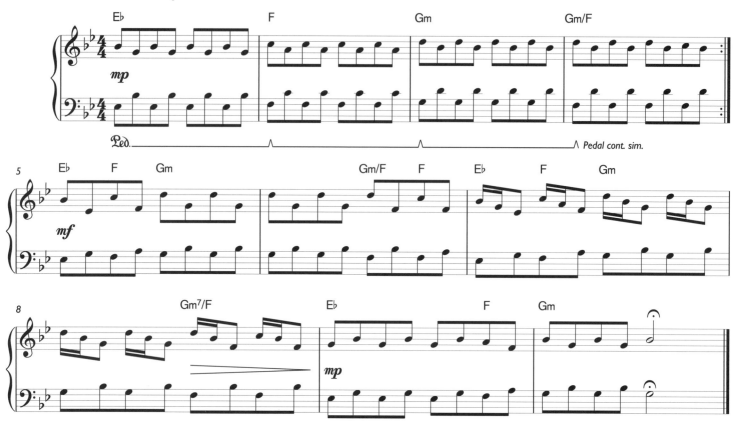

14.

This piece is good for developing a steady left hand.
It provides an introduction to three of the basic stylistic factors of disco:
syncopation, frequent seventh and ninth chords and a strong turnaround.

♩ = 116 **Disco**

15.

A simple study to demonstrate how to build up a piece using the left hand alone.
The right-hand pattern is the same throughout, with the left hand simply building up
through the different note lengths. Get gradually louder as the study progresses.

16.

This study can feel quite fast, so practise it slowly at first then build up speed.
Many storytelling singer-songwriters compose in 3 time: check out Billy Joel, Rufus Wainwright and Leonard Cohen.

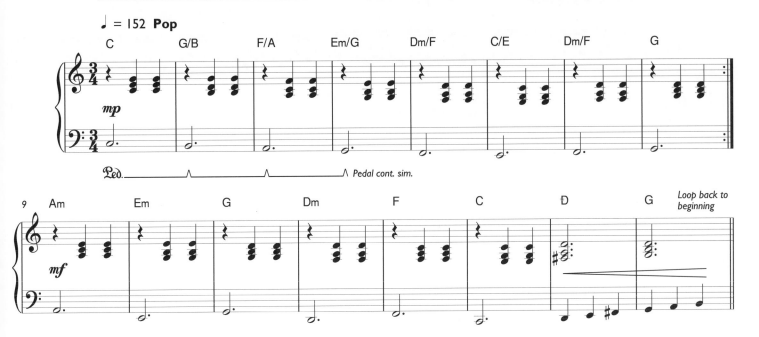

17.

Make sure you can play the left-hand arpeggio patterns smoothly and evenly before adding the right-hand melody. This is a great technique to master as it creates a complete accompaniment on its own leaving the right hand free to play chords or a melody line.

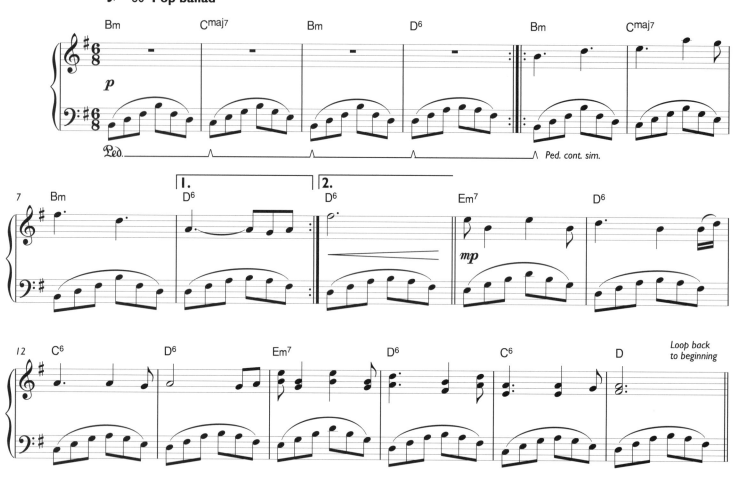

18.

This is a commonly used example of an intro to a pop ballad. It has a descending semiquaver part in the right hand and a simple chordal left hand line. Don't rush it.

19.

The stressed notes in the left hand give a clear beat in this piece.
It can be tricky to get your fingers around the hymnal chords in bars 6 and 8,
so practise those separately. Really build up the crescendo in the final section.

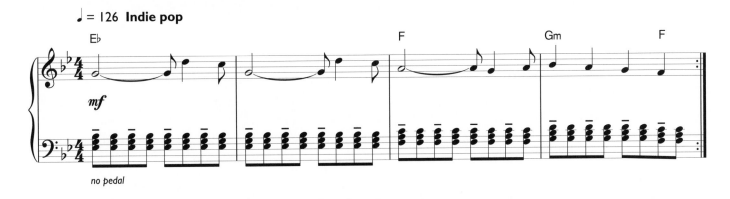
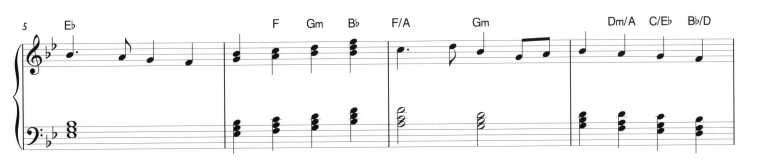
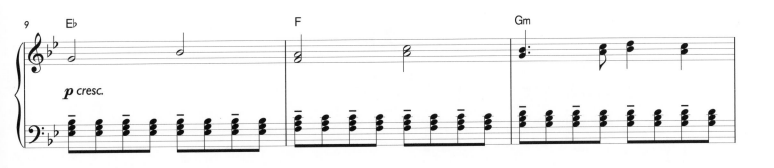
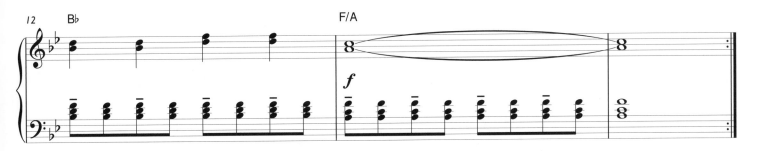

20.

You'll probably recognise this right-hand rhythm from the countless indie pop bands that have used it over the years. Keep it dancey, especially when the left hand kicks in with the straight crotchets towards the end. If you can play them as octaves it'll sound stronger still.

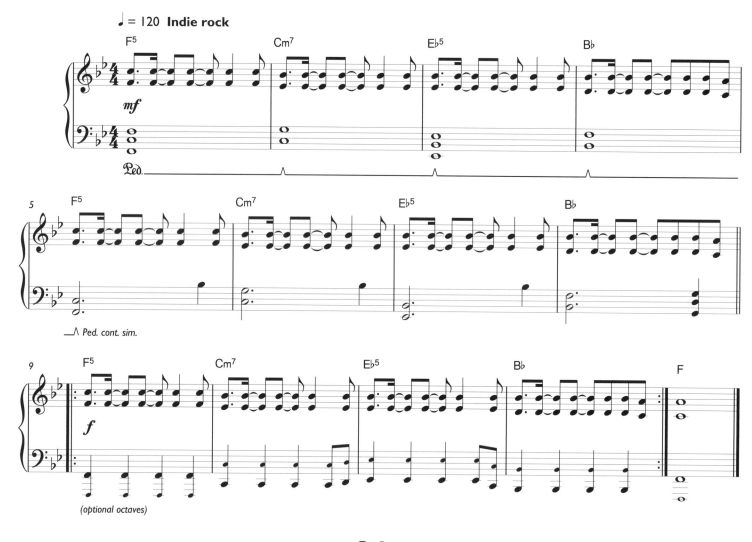

(optional octaves)

21.

Both hands play syncopated rhythms together in this study.
Playing along to a metronome or beat will help you keep in time.

22.

This is a guitar-style study, reminiscent of modern indie tunes.
Play really lightly, making sure that both hands are completely together.
In the second section, the right hand pre-empts the chord with a sharp stab.
Try to make this strong whilst keeping the other chords very staccato.

♩ = 104 **Indie rock**

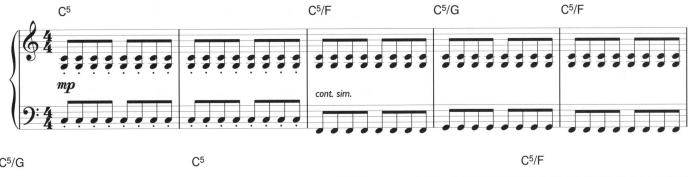

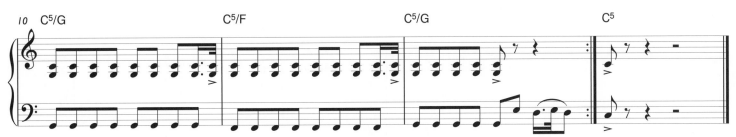

23.

This pattern and chord progression has been used in a multitude of songs over the decades.
Try to make little rhythmic adjustments to both hands when you feel confident, but start by keeping
it steady and light. You can increase the speed as much as you like when you know the pattern.

♩ = 80 **Rock**

24.

A commonly used effect in pop piano playing is to have both hands in the treble clef.
Check out piano songs from Regina Spektor, Kate Bush, Tom Odell and Alicia Keys for inspiration.

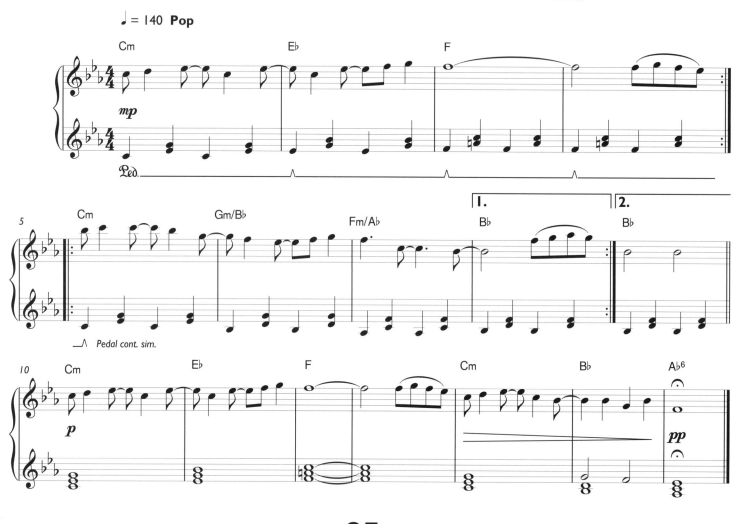

25.

There are literally hundreds of pop ballads that use this right-hand pattern as the basis of the song.
Both hands should play smoothly and fairly freely you can pull the tempo around a little in keeping with the piece.

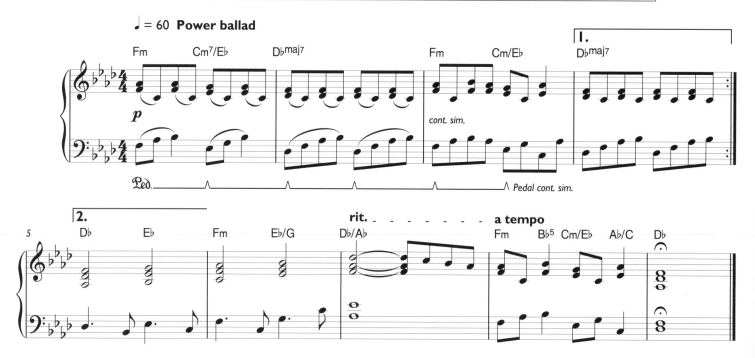

26.

Try counting out the quavers as 123 123 12, accenting all the '1's to get this pattern spot on.
This rhythm is used in many pop songs, such as 'Clocks' by Coldplay.

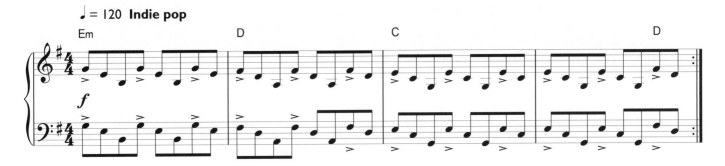

27.

In this study there are three devices that are frequently found in pop songs. The first is starting quietly and high up in the piano range; the second is using a repeating riff over a different bass note; the third is creating a build-up, which is the way to get a crowd going at a live gig. Play the first 8 bars gently and lightly, then go for it when the bass properly kicks in.

28.

A solid driving bass with big chords in the right hand gives a great intro to many songs.
This is typical of rap and trip-hop genres. Keep the bassline steady and the right-hand chords strong.
Watch out in the last four bars as the right hand goes into the bass clef for the outro.

29.

A trademark reggae study with right-hand chords on the off-beat and a typical bassline.
Reggae is slower than you might think, so don't rush, keep it laid back and set your metronome if necessary.

30.

This rhythm is typical of an 80s rock style. Be sure to bring out the off-beat accents in the left hand as they mark a change in bass note.

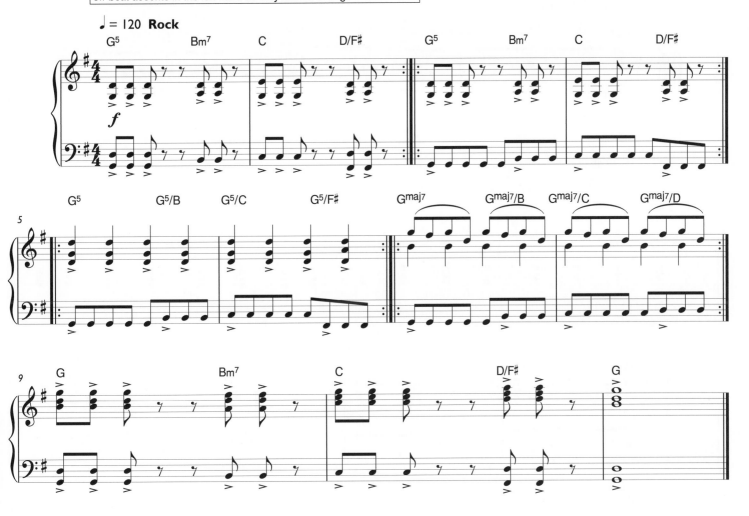

31.

Quite a lot of 'showy' pop songs use this time signature as it can create a dramatic effect. This study needs to be played with strength in the left hand and really bringing out the bassline and playing each quaver in the right hand evenly. You might find it helpful to count the nine quavers in the bar as you play.

32.

Look out for the accented notes in this study, they need to be played clearly and louder than the other notes.
The left-hand part gradually builds up throughout the study, creating momentum.

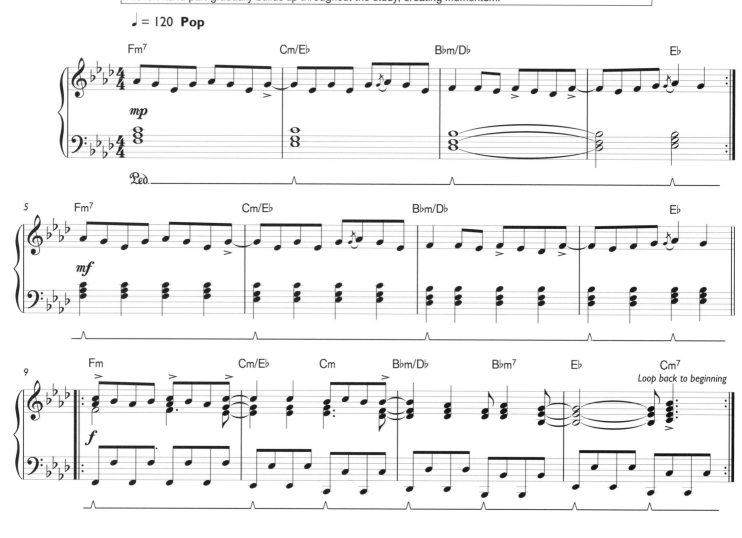

33.

It's possible to create an effective pop groove using just two chords. Here, both hands are playing
in the bass clef. The left hand keeps the beat and the right hand creates the rhythmic element.
The chords build in the right hand: develop this in your own way, it's a good starting point for an improvisation.

34.

This study is in a folk pop style. The chord names should help you sight-read it.
Play gently, make a note of the pedalling and watch out for the $\frac{3}{8}$ bars.

♩. = 60 **Folk pop ballad**

35.

This study has a classical style that is used by many songwriters for their rock & pop ballads.
The piece should be awash with pedal at the start, then from bar 5 you should bring
out the accented notes in the right hand to create a melody above the arpeggios.

♩. = 60 **Classical pop ballad**

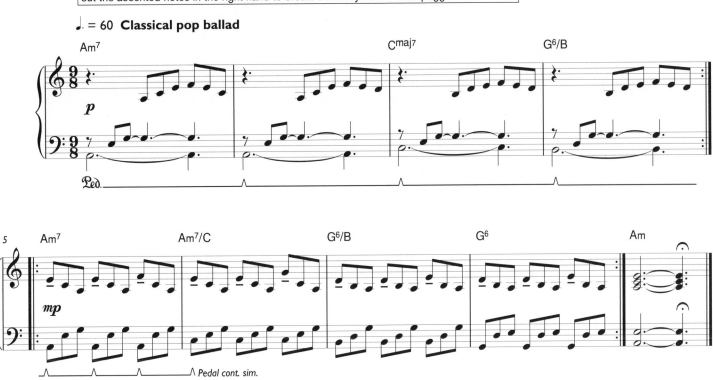

36.

As pop piano players we often have to emultate the sounds of other instruments in order to recreate different styles. In this study we're emulating an acoustic guitar finger-picking style of playing, which can sound quite effective on the piano. Try to imitate an acoustic guitarist playing this.

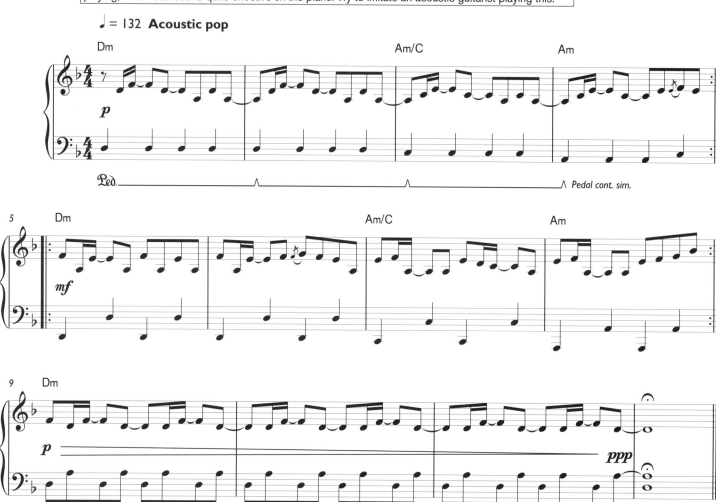

37.

This is a classic chord sequence with some straightforward syncopation every second bar. You'll have probably heard this style in many songs, old and new! Keep the left hand light.

38.

Don't be put off by the right-hand rhythm, it looks more complicated than it actually is, and it should sound familiar to you. This rhythm creates the dance feel of the song. Take it slowly to start with and count against the straight left-hand crotchets. In this tune some bars are in 2, which emphasise the chord changes.

39.

The main riff of this piece is totally syncopated but the steady crotchets in the left hand should help you count the rhythm. This study is typical of a pop ballad where there's a short melody with a chordal part beneath.

40.

This study uses a mix of time signatures, so count carefully. These changes in time emphasise the descending pattern. There are some interesting chords used here which might inspire you to go on and write your own pieces. Notice that both hands are playing in the treble clef.

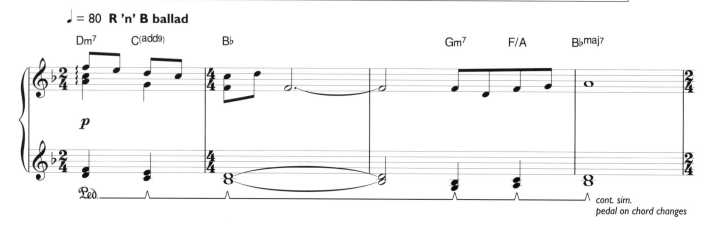

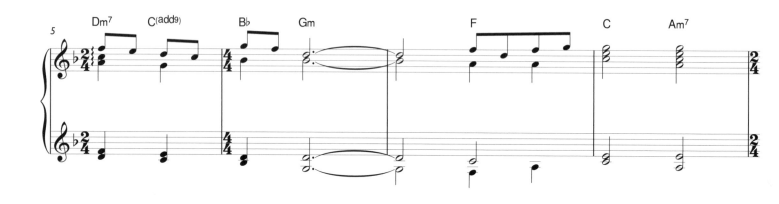

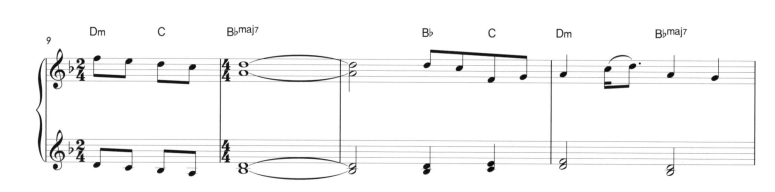

41.

This is a study using syncopation, left-hand chords, sustain pedal and typical R 'n' B ballad harmonies. Check out songs by Sam Smith, Labrinth and Sampha for more inspiration.

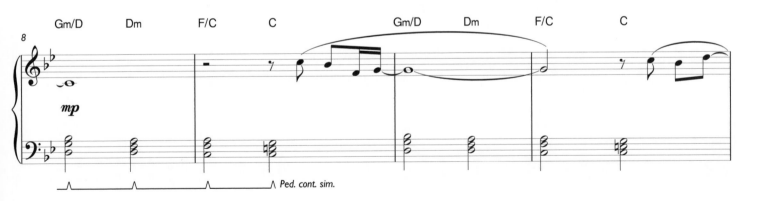

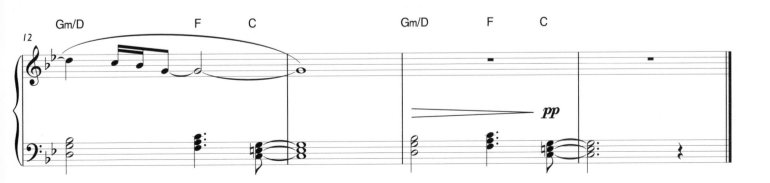

42.

You might want to play this bassline through first before adding the right-hand melody.
Boogie woogie is a style of music which was at its height in the 1920s and the bass pattern
is a great one to master, leaving your right hand free to improvise a melody.

♩ = 120 **Boogie woogie**

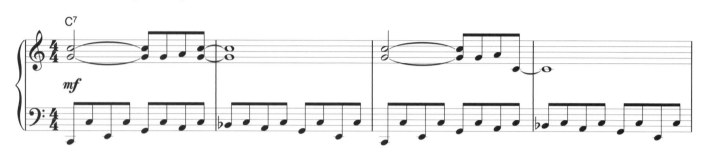

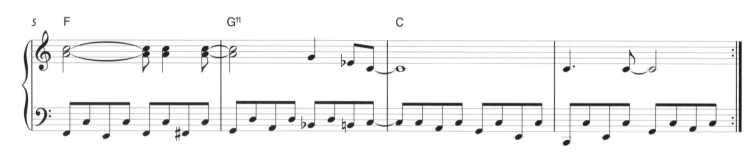

43.

There are similarities between this ska study and the previous reggae tunes, but ska has a much faster tempo.
Because of the speed and the repeating bass notes, you shouldn't need to use the pedal.

♩ = 144 **Ska**

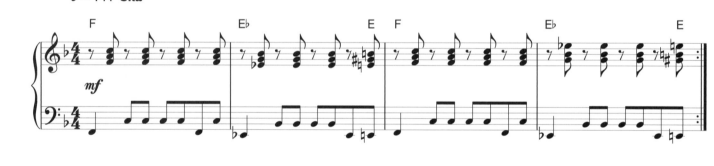

44.

Get used to keeping the quavers in the right hand smooth and steady
and the left-hand semiquavers light and short.

♩ = 72 **Pop**

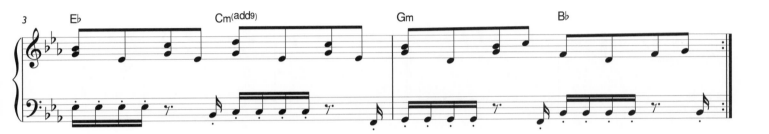

45.

This study is a great way of getting a steady walking bass
going whilst holding down a melody in the right hand.

♩ = 100 **Swung, relaxed blues**

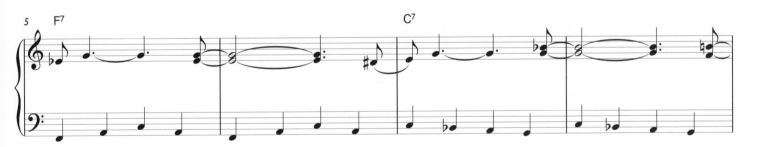

46.

Play this bass groove with strength, but keep the right hand rhythmic and light when it comes in.
Make sure you follow the accent and staccato markings. For further listening check out Stevie Wonder and Michael Jackson.

47.

Playing a melody line in both hands can sound really powerful when harmonised.
Here, the left-hand part is much more than a rhythmic accompaniment as it has
the melody line (in unison with the right hand) whilst also holding the root pulse.

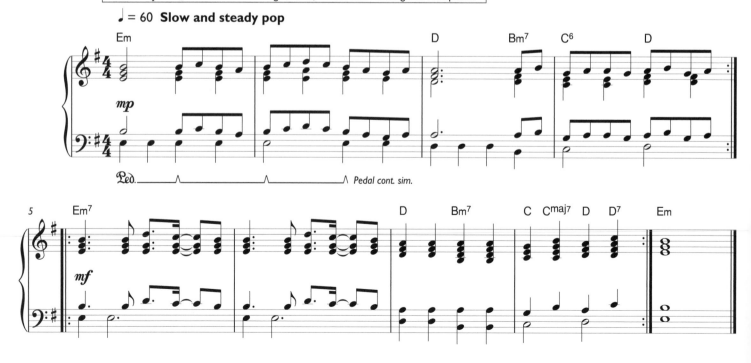

48.

A study designed to strengthen the left hand, particuarly in carrying the driving rhythmic patterns. Four typical styles of left-hand accompaniment patterns are used. Repeat each one as many times as you need to practise it.

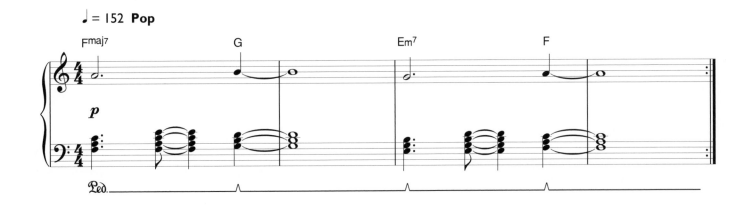

49.

This piece is based on a traditional folk melody called 'False, False'. It's a great introduction to playing in a folk-style, with typical elements such as grace notes and flourishes in bars 3 and 11. As it's a folk piece, don't feel restricted by the tempo, pull it around as you see fit. You can also just play the left hand on the repeat and improvise your own melody over the top. Check out folk acts such as The Unthanks, Seth Lakeman and Capercaillie for further listening.

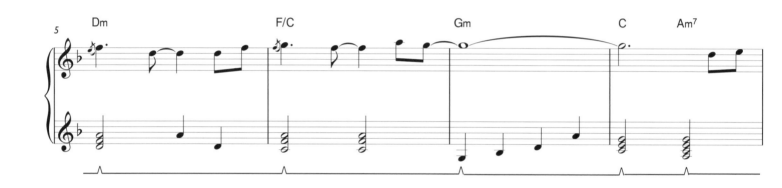

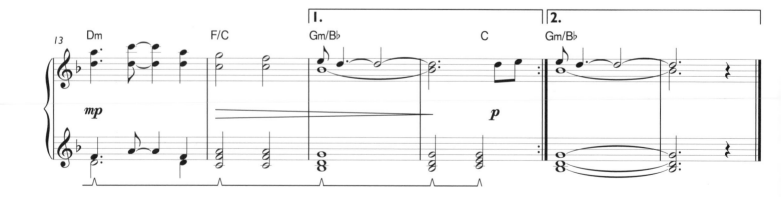

50.

You can either count this in 3 (minims) or 6 (crotchets). As the majority of chord changes are on the last two beats of the bar, it has a 4 + 2 feel as well, which is a common device in pop and dance music.

51.

Only octaves are used in this study, so it's all about the rhythm. Keep the right hand very light. If you're playing a synth you might want to experiment with using different sounds.

52.

Dance music is characterised by a fairly fast BPM, repeating musical phrases and a form that clearly builds up and down throughout.
Here, the build up is created through the momentum of the bass-line, with a right-hand chord pattern that is typical of this genre.
Check out tunes from Calvin Harris, Avicii and Röyksopp for good examples of the style.

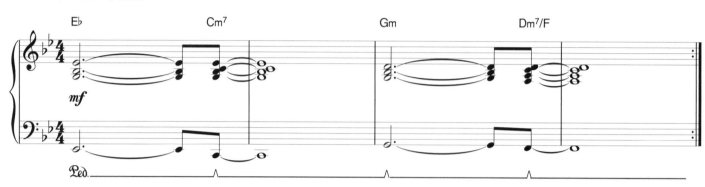

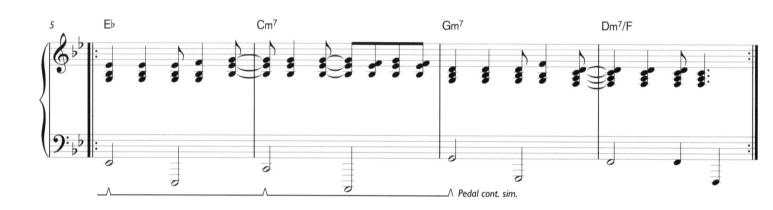

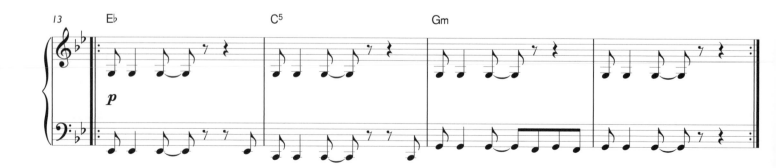

53.

Your right and left hands play this rock-style riff an octave apart; a great technique to use if you want to give power to a riff.
To end this study, finish on another trademark of classic rock, the power chord, where only the root and fifth notes are played.

54.

A classic way for a dance pop song to start: big loud chords that really stretch your hands, then a rhythmic pattern which leads on to a build up. Make the most of the accented note in bars 3 and 11, they're a common feature of this style.

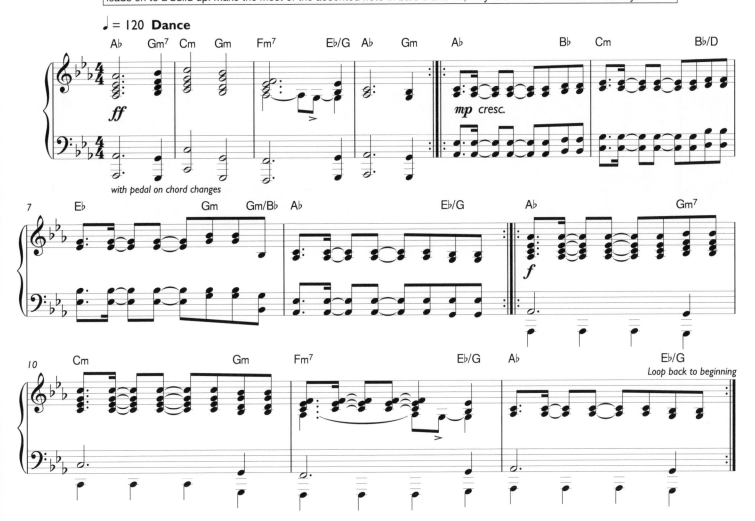

55.

This piece is reminiscent of much guitar pop music from Mali.
Short melodies come at the end of each bar and a clear rhythm drives the piece.
Check out Tinariwen and Amadou & Mariam for more inspiration.

♩ = 100 **African pop**

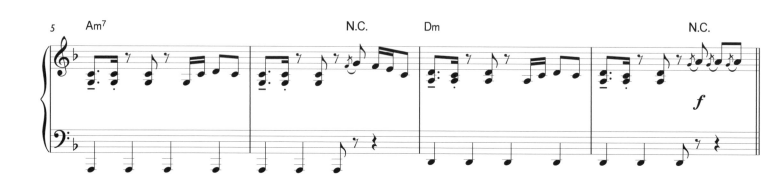

56.

This is a sequence typical of a gospel style in 3, with cross-overs into soul and pop music.
The triplet sections can appear difficult to understand, so try to feel this rather than be
too restricted by the notation: it looks more complex than it actually is!

57.

This study will help you get used to typical funk synchronisation styles and harmonies.
You should work on making this as natural-sounding as possible so it sits easily in the groove.

58.

Make sure you nail the rhythm in the left hand in the first four bars.
There are lots of repeating notes in the right hand of this study;
make sure each one is clearly heard.

♩ = 130 **Folk pop**

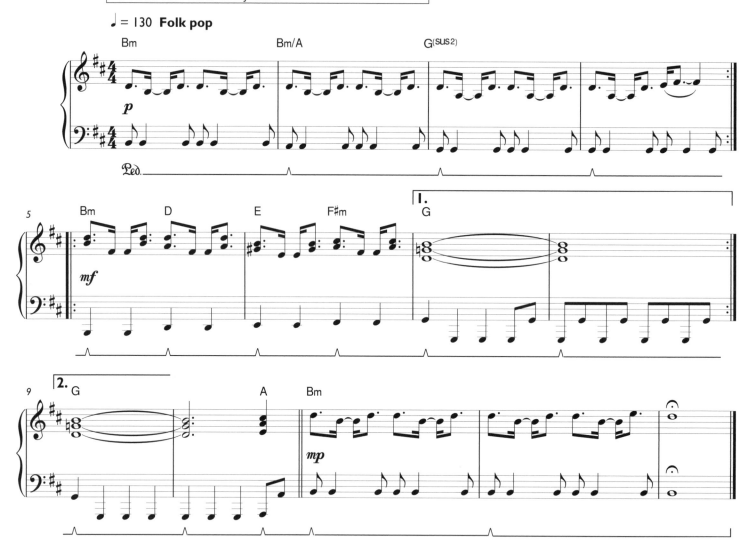

59.

This funky pop bass-line should be played steadily, with clears rests to give it the funk-pop sound.
The right-hand accented chords emphasise the off-beat.

♩ = 120 **Funk pop**

60.

This dance study demonstrates subtle changes to the harmony can change a piece.
There are typical elements of trance music here, with build-ups, a breakdown and a driving rhythmic pattern.

61.

A straight-forward rhythmic exercise designed to practise playing lightly
with both hands. It might be useful to play with a metronome the first few times.

62.

Right-hand chord changes over an unchanging root note can sound really effective.
Make sure you keep the staccato chords really light and the bass rhythm steady and consistent.

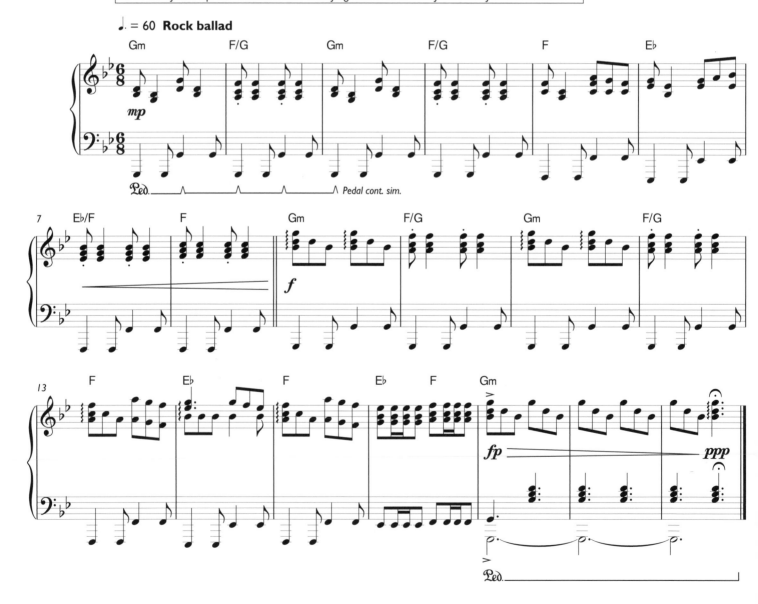

63.

This chromatic chord sequence has hints of the James Bond theme about it.
Keep the 12312312 quaver rhythm going steadily throughout the first two sections.

64.

This study demonstrates a good way to build up some basic country licks whilst rocking out.
Check out songs from Billy Ray Cyrus, Sheryl Crow and Garth Brooks.

38

65.

A great study for hand synchronisation and developing power in repeated notes. Gradually speed it up until it becomes thrash metal. Can you handle 200 bpm?! Check out Dream Theater and Dragonforce for further listening.

♩ = 120 **Brutal metal**

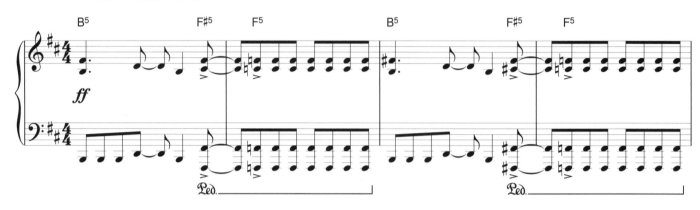

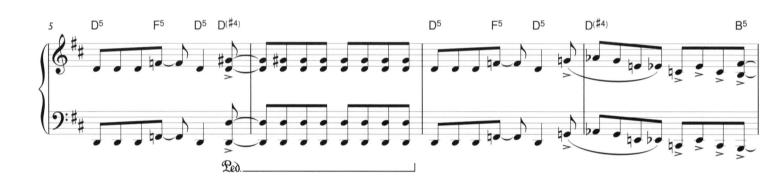

66.

At the start, this piece could be mistaken for a straight tune in 4,
but the compound quadruple time kicks in with the swung bass from bar 7.
Check out songs by Disclosure and Mary J. Blige for more inspiration.

67.

The right hand leads the pattern here which can feel odd, and can really change the feel of a piece. Play both hands very lightly and increase the speed when you feel confident. The study travels through different keys which is typical of a progressive rock style, as are the classical/romantic undertones.

♩ = 100 **Proggressive rock**

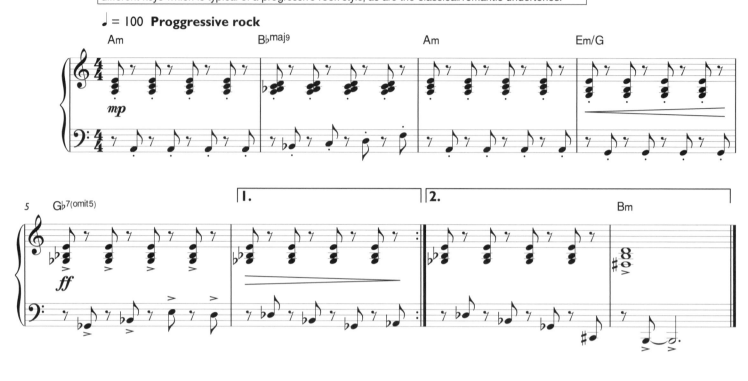

68.

This gospel exercise practises driving the song from the bass. Try playing several times with increasing improvisation in the right hand, whilst keeping the bass solid. Don't rush and keep the groove laid-back.

♩ = 138 **Gospel/soul, with swung quavers**

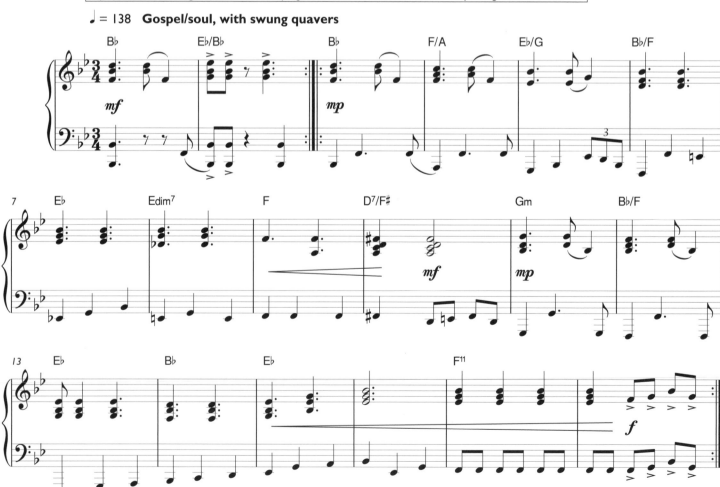

69.

Don't be put off by the key signature, flat keys have wonderful tonal qualities, and playing in this key high in the piano with lots of sustain gives a lovely effect. This study is an example of a pop ballad intro and should be played freely.

70.

The whole range of the keyboard is often put to use in rock 'n' roll music, so your hands end up quite far apart. If you're feeling adventurous try the right-hand an octave higher still. Make sure it is playing lightly so that each semiquaver is really short. The bassline should be steady and clear. There's a glissando at the end of bar 6: play this with the whole of your thumbnail, giving yourself enough time to get back to the C chord at the start of the piece. Listen to classic Rock 'n' roll songs from Jerry Lee Lewis, Elvis Presley, Fats Domino and Chuck Berry for inspiration.

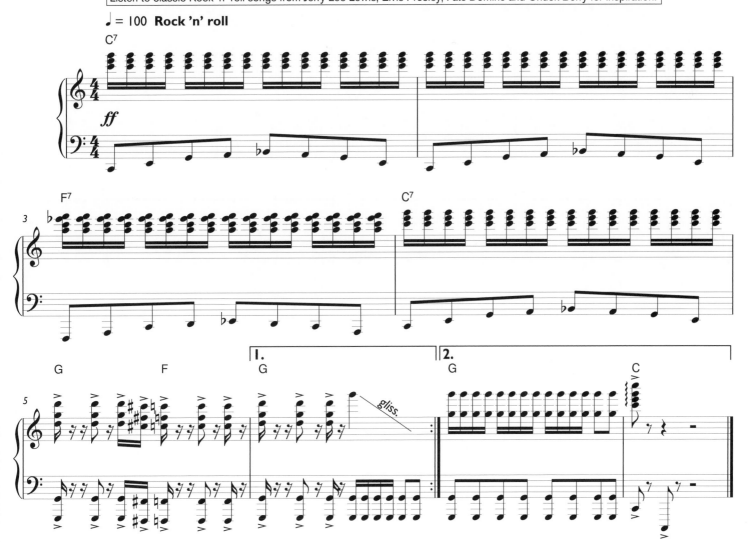

71.

This study is fast and should be awash with the sustain pedal. It's designed
to help you practise keeping hands exactly together. Keep both hands
completely unified and flowing then, if you can, speed the pattern up.

♩ = 168 **Rock intro**

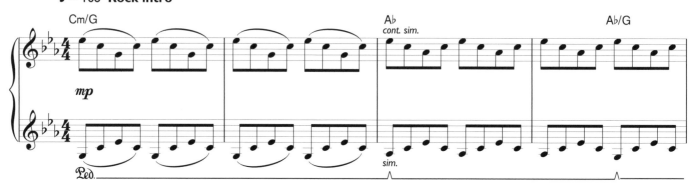

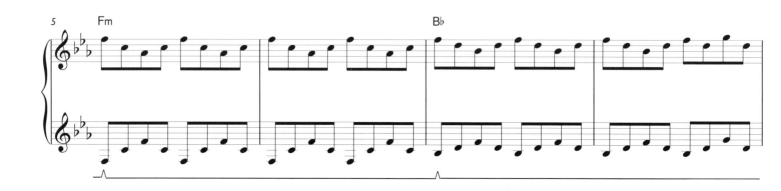

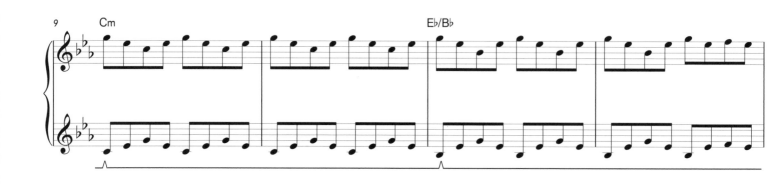

72.

A disco study designed to make the distinction between the staccato left-hand pattern, with the varying right-hand part. Don't vary the tempo at all, the left hand should be constant throughout. Try playing with a metronome at first.

♩ = 120 **Disco**

73.

This study is very much driven by the left-hand bassline, so keep that the focal point of the piece.

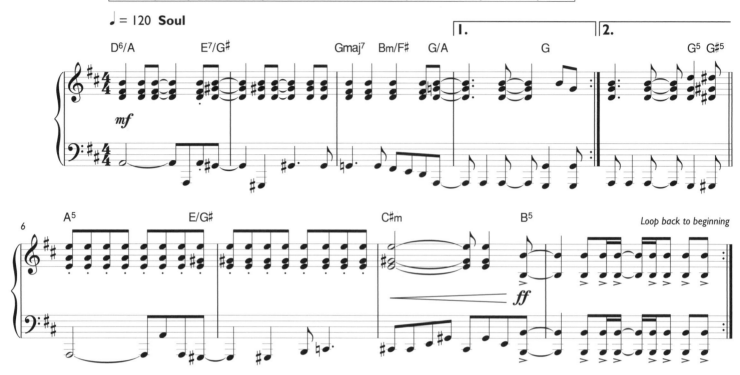

74.

Observe all the rests in this study: it should played lightly and rhythmically at all times.
Although the rhythm may look complex, it's actually fairly straight-forward and is a classic dance pattern.

75.

Play with a very slight swing and try to sit a bit behind the beat.
Make sure you keep the bass firm and steady, and the right hand light.

♩ = 80 **Reggae**

76.

Here we have a study where the right hand is smooth and repetitive, with off-beat fifths in the left hand.
This can create a really great effect, especially when the left hand goes back on the beat in bars 3 and 6.

♩ = 100 **Rock**

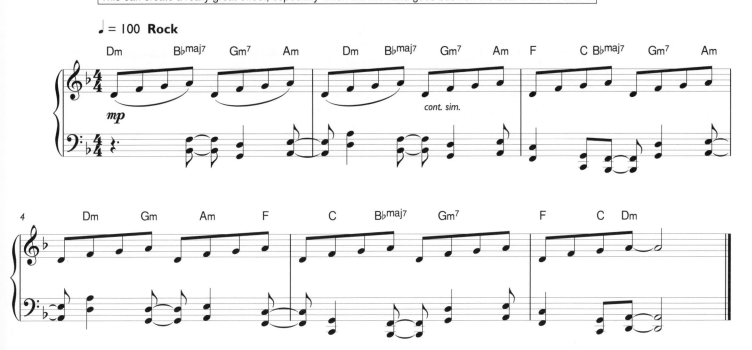

77.

A good study in a soul/Motown style, ideal for practising syncopation and rapid unison riffs.
Check out songs by The Jackson 5, Stevie Wonder, Martha & The Vandellas and The Supremes.

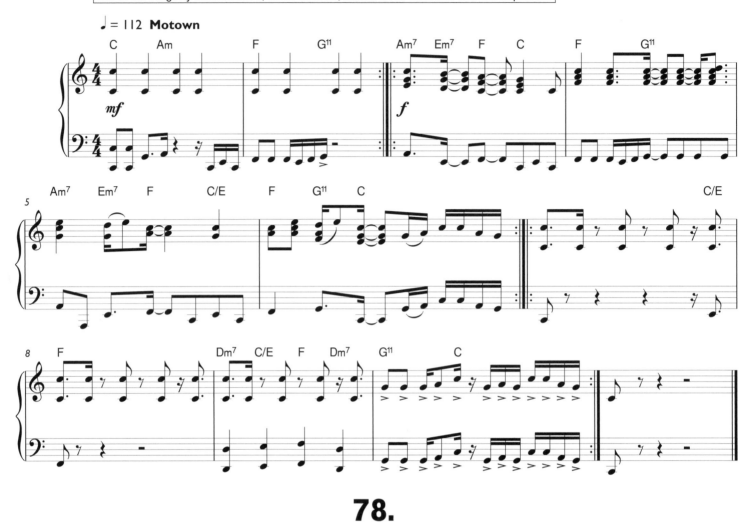

78.

This is a bass solo designed to give the left hand a work-out, whilst retaining a basic chordal acompaniment above.
Check out tunes by Parliament, Sly & The Family Stone, Funkadelic and The Average White Band for further listening.

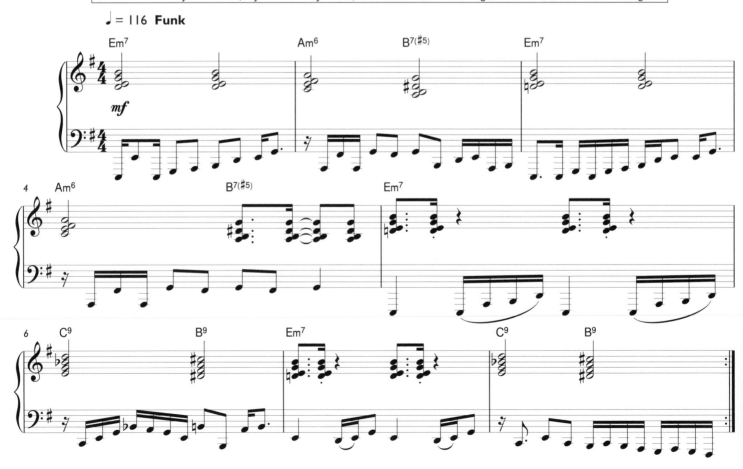

79.

This 12-bar blues study takes you through several improvisation patterns to a typical turnaround.
Listen to songs by Ray Charles and Fats Domino to help you nail this style.

♩ = 76 **Swung: slow and lazy blues**

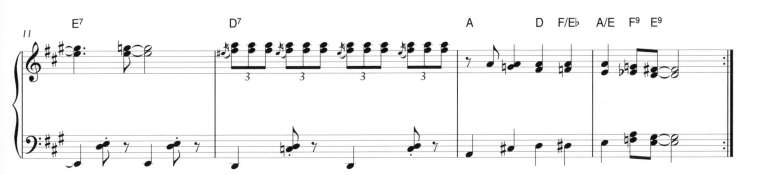

80.

Designed to develop rhythmic interplay between the hands, this study should be nice and light. Check out bands like Duran Duran, Spandau Ballet and The Human League for more playing ideas.

81.

A great study for practising intricate, atonal metal riffs in the left hand.
Take it slower if you can't manage this tempo, then speed up a little.

♩. = 144 **Metal**

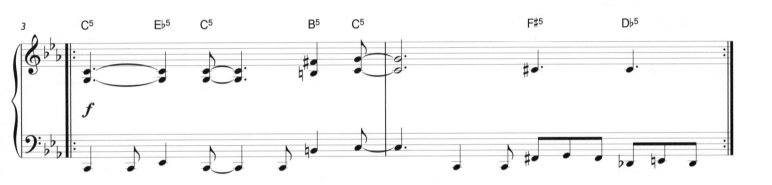

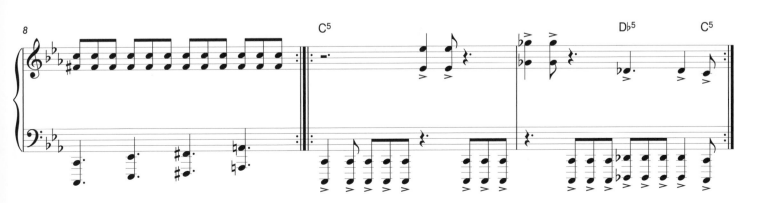

82.

This should get you used to a lot of Rock 'n' roll piano tricks.
Always play with aplomb, in the right hand there can be no wrong notes!
Pick any high note to start your glissando on in bar 9.

♩ = 152 **Rock 'n' roll**

83.

Playing in 5 can completely change the feel of rock & pop music and can create interesting and original sounding songs.
Count out the rhythm first and repeat the first two bars as many times as it takes to nail the rhythm.

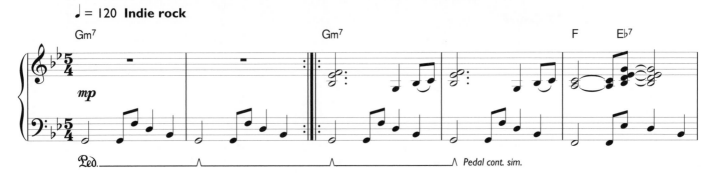

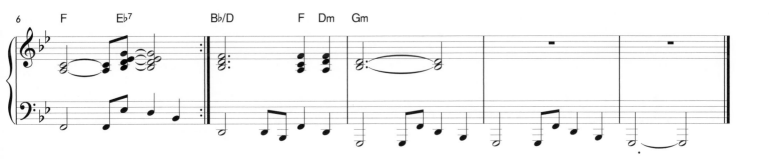

84.

In this study, you'll need to play the bass semibreve then immediately move your hand into another position to play the rest of the arpeggio.
The sustain pedal will keep the root note ringing. The right hand is a simple line, so you can concentrate on playing the arpeggios accurately.

52

85.

Play this dance/pop study as lightly as possible at the
beginning and end, with a little more force in the middle.

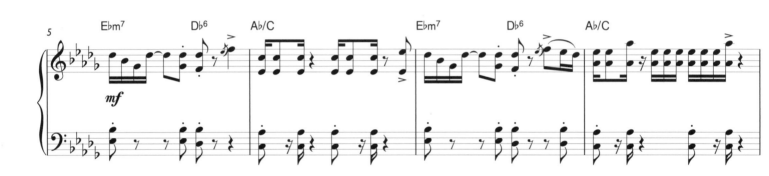

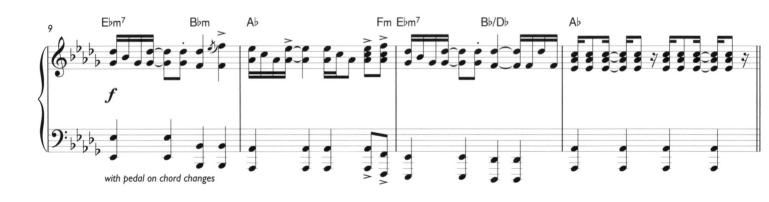

86.

This is a good study for getting your hands around the thick chords and rapid runs
common in more poppy styles of disco music, whilst keeping a steady beat in the left hand.
Check out songs by Donna Summer, the Bee Gees and Earth, Wind & Fire for further listening.

54

87.

Take care to make sure that the melody comes out clearly whilst keeping the quavers flowing.
This piece is good for practising your parallel octaves and arpeggios. Pay particular care to the dynamics.

88.

On the more progressive/melodic side of metal, this final study is designed to practise a few
keyboard equivalents of metal solo techniques. Look out for the sweep-picking/arpeggios at bar 5.
If you're on a keyboard, try a hammond organ patch with a little distortion.

PIANO SONGBOOKS
FROM FABER MUSIC

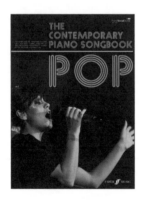  

To buy Faber Music publications or to find out about the full range of titles available
please contact your local music retailer or Faber Music sales enquiries:

Faber Music Ltd, Burnt Mill, Elizabeth Way, Harlow CM20 2HX
Tel: +44 (0) 1279 82 89 82   Fax: +44 (0) 1279 82 89 83
sales@fabermusic.com   fabermusicstore.com